# INSTANT BOOKKEEPING

By Darlyne C. Conway

Printed and Published in U.S.A. By

*Educator Books, Inc.*

DRAWER 32 SAN ANGELO, TEXAS 76901

I

To

Brenda and Kyle

# TABLE OF CONTENTS

# INTRODUCTION

Bookkeeping records are an essential and vital part of any business; without them a business could not function for any great length of time. This book provides a simple and practical way to set up a small set of books that any businessman or housewife can use.

There is no mystery to bookkeeping. After learning a few logical rules and applying them to everyday business transactions, one can become so acquainted with the subject that it becomes a profitable habit. It is as easy as learning a simple game of cards. One can learn bookkeeping by watching how it is done and "Learn to Do By Doing". Study each illustration and explanation that is given until you fully understand it.

Bookkeeping is also useful in planning future operations. By comparing the most recent month with the preceding month and with the preceding year, it becomes apparent what the trend is. By further analyzation, it will be possible to see what is really making a profit or what is causing the business to lose money.

In order to obtain credit a business usually has to provide a financial statement and with a simple set of books you can have a statement in no time at all.

Also, there are certain Federal, State and Local Government reports a business is required to prepare and a keeping of records is necessary. Even for the housewife keeping records can make the Federal Income Tax report so much easier to figure each year.

The most modern means of bookkeeping is called the double-entry system. This means that for every business transaction there are two entries; one which is known as a debit, the other as a credit. Hence, all debit entries must balance with all credit entries providing a means of proof. In double entry, the first recording is the entering of a transaction in the respective Journal and the second recording is to the Ledger.

The principle Journals are:
1. Cash Receipts (receiving of cash)
2. Sales Journal (selling)
3. Purchase Journal (buying)
4. Cash Disbursements Journal (payments by check)
5. General Journal (miscellaneous transactions)

In the following chapters, you will see how each of these Journals is used with easy to understand illustrations.

The bookkeeper's work is to record any transaction that occurs into one of these journals listed above. At the end of each month, the columns of each of these books are totaled and the totals transferred to the General Ledger. The General Ledger is used as the basic record in which the effects of business transactions are classified and summarized. Turn to Chapter X for a more detailed description of the use of the General Ledger.

# DICTIONARY OF WORDS USED BY THE BOOKKEEPER

| | |
|---|---|
| ACCOUNT | A form of record used for each individual item |
| ASSETS | The properties that a business owns |
| BALANCE | Debits equal the credits |
| CAPITAL | Amount which it takes to get the business started or to continue; also known as Net Worth. The difference between the Assets and Liabilities is the Net Worth |
| CREDIT | An entry that is a credit to an account |
| DEBIT | An entry that is a charge to an account |
| ENTRY | Recording a transaction |
| FISCAL | Annual bookkeeping period |
| JOURNAL | A book in which a business transaction is first entered |
| LEDGER | A book to which a business transaction is posted after having first been entered in a Journal. In the Ledger there is a page for each account |
| LIABILITIES | List of the business debts |
| POSTING | Entering what is transcribed on the Journals to the respective Ledgers |

# CHAPTER I

## ACCOUNTS RECEIVABLE LEDGER

In almost every business there is an Accounts Receivable unless all the transactions are cash sales and no charges. The Accounts Receivable is a ledger with a page in alphabetical order for each customer that has bought on credit. It is a record of sales to the customer and payments received from the customer.

At the time the merchandise is bought, the salesman writes the name and address of the customer on the invoice (sales slip) and fills it out properly with all the merchandise listed and the amount charged. He will give a copy of the invoice to the customer and the original invoice will be given to the bookkeeper for entering. The bookkeeper enters the invoice in the Sales Journal showing the date, customers' name, invoice number and the amount of the invoice. (Explanation in detail on this is found in Chapter III). From the Sales Journal the bookkeeper posts to the customer's page in the Accounts Receivable Ledger showing the same information along with the page number of the Sales Journal from which the amount of the invoice was posted. Place a check mark (√) by the side of the amount in the Sales Journal to signify it has been posted to the Accounts Receivable. When posting from the Sales Journal to the Accounts Receivable Ledger the amount is entered in the debit column and extended over to the balance column. If there is a previous balance, each time a charge is made the invoice amount is added to the balance total.

Study the illustration given below and learn what we have covered so far.

| | | | | | | | | | | |
|---|---|---|---|---|---|---|---|---|---|---|
| | | | | | | | | | | |
| Date | | | Post. Ref. | Debit | | Credit | | | Balance | |
| 1969 8 5 | Inv #517 | | 5549 | 5 | 95 | | | | 5 | 95 |
| 8 17 | Inv #725 | | 5553 | 113 | 49 | | | | 119 | 44 |
| | | | | | | | | | | |
| | | Sum of both entries in debit column ⤴ | | | | | | | | |

*Customers' Name + Address*

When a customer sends in a payment on account, the bookkeeper enters in the Cash Receipts Journal the date payment was received, name of customer, and the amount received. (Explanation in detail on this is found in Chapter IV.) The bookkeeper then posts from the Cash Receipts Journal to the customers' page in the Accounts Receivable the same information along with the page number of the Cash Receipts Journal from which the amount of the payment was posted. Place a check mark (√) by the side of the amount in the Cash Receipts Journal to signify that it has been posted. This amount is entered in the credit column and subtracted from the balance total. If the balance is paid in full show a zero or a sign -0-.

Now study the illustration given that shows what we have covered to this point.

| Customer's Name & Address | | | | | |
|---|---|---|---|---|---|
| Date | | Post ref. | Debit | Credit | Balance |
| 8 5 | Inv # 517 | SJ49 | 5 95 | | 5 95 |
| 17 | Inv # 520 | SJ49 | 113 49 | | 119 44 |
| 20 | | CR26 | | 50 00 | 69 44 |
| 9 10 | | CR39 | | 69 44 | -0- |

this was subtracted from 119.44 balance to get

and this reduced balance to

At the end of the month, if a customer owes anything, a monthly statement should be mailed to him showing what his charges and credits were for the current month. Statement forms already printed can be purchased at office supply firms or if you desire, statments can be printed according to your specifications by a printing shop.

A sample of a statement is illustrated.

## Statement

### BUSINESS FIRM'S NAME
### & ADDRESS

To:   Customer's Name
      & Address

Month:   August

| Date | Invoice No. | Charge | | Credit | | Balance | |
|------|-------------|--------|---|--------|---|---------|---|
| 8 5 | 517 | 5 | 95 | | | 5 | 95 |
| 8 17 | 520 | 113 | 49 | | | 119 | 44 |
| 8 20 | | | | 50 | 00 | 69 | 44 |
| | | | | | | | |
| | | | | | | | |
| | | | | | | | |
| | | | | | | | |
| | | | | | | | |

Also, at the end of the month when all customers sales and payments have been entered in the Accounts Receivable Ledger to their respective pages, an adding machine tape should be run on all accounts with a balance. When the tape is accurately run and totaled, attach it to the front of the ledger to hold until all the books have been balanced for the month. The total on the tape should balance out with the total that appears on the Accounts Receivable Account sheet in the General Ledger. If it does not agree and the mistake is not in the tape, all postings will have to be rechecked until the error is found.

Sometime during the month a list should be made of the delinquent accounts for the collection department. This list should include the customers' name, amount and length of time owing.

The Accounts Receivable has valuable information on it. A quick glance through the pages can tell a businessman who are his best customers and which ones he needs to call on to build up sales.

# CHAPTER II

## ACCOUNTS PAYABLE LEDGER

The Accounts Payable is a ledger for recording the business transactions with creditors. The bills that are received for merchandise purchased and services performed are recorded first in the Purchase Journal and then posted to the individual, alphabetized, creditor's page in the Accounts Payable Ledger as a credit (See illustration). The payments made on these bills are first recorded in the Cash Disbursement Journal (see Chapter VI) and then posted to the creditors' page as a debit. (See illustration). A check mark (√) should be made by the amount in the Cash Disbursements Journal signifying it has been posted just as you have done with the Accounts Receivable. The balance column on the creditor's page will have a credit balance when the posting is made from the Purchase Journal; this amount should be shown in red ink or have brackets around it.

At the end of the month run an adding machine tape on the balances and this total should balance with the total in the General Ledger.

A list of the balances should be made showing what creditors you still owe for how much and how long. This accounts payable is an important part to the businessman. It keeps him informed as to what extent he is in debt. The Accounts Payable should never exceed the Accounts Receivable for that would mean he would have more to pay out than he would have coming in.

| Creditors Name | | | | | |
| + Address | | | | | |
| Date | | Post Ref. | Debit | Credit | Balance |
| 8 31 | | PJ 8 | | 95 70 | ⟨95 70⟩ |
| 9 10 | | CD 8 | 95 70 | | —0— |
| | | | | | |
| | | | | | |
| | | | | | |
| | | | | | |

4

# CHAPTER III

## SALES JOURNAL

The Sales Journal is used solely for recording sales of merchandise on account. Sales of merchandise for cash are recorded in the cash receipts journal. Sales of assets or of any other nature that does not pertain to stock in trade are recorded in either the cash receipts journal or the general journal.

When a copy of the sales invoice is received by the bookkeeper, she enters it in numerical order in the **Sales Journal** with the following information.

1. Date of invoice
2. Customer's name
3. Invoice number
4. Amount of invoice

Study the illustration given below.

| SJ 49 | Sales Journal August, 19— | | | | | |
|---|---|---|---|---|---|---|
| Date | Name | Inv. no. | Accts Rec. - Dr. Sales - Cr | | | |
| 8  3 | Seth Roberts | 516 | 10 95 ✓ | | | |
| 5 | Bill's Repair Shop | 517 | 5 95 ✓ | | | |
| 10 | Cycle Service | 518 | 32 50 ✓ | | | |
| 15 | Dale Roberts | 519 | 157 00 ✓ | | | |
| 17 | Bill's Repair Shop | 520 | 113 49 ✓ | | | |
| 20 | Grant Cole | 521 | 65 23 ✓ | | | |
| 25 | Henry Andrews | 522 | 55 00 ✓ | | | |
| 31 | Lambert's Toy Store | 523 | 512 00 ✓ | | | |
| | Total | | 952 12 | | | |

Each entry in the sales journal is posted as a debit to the appropriate account in the Accounts Receivable Ledger. These should be posted daily so the customer's account can be determined at all times. At the time the posting is made to the customer's account, a check (√) is placed by the side of the amount as it is shown in our illustration. This indicates that the item has been posted and requires no further attention. Also, when posting show the initial of the journal you are working in and the page number (refer to page 2 in Posting Reference column).

The preceding illustration shows all sales in one column although it is necessary for some companies to distribute in one or more columns the various items on each invoice to provide sales information.

Study the illustration below:

**SJ 49**

## Sales Journal
### August, 19 ___

| Date | Name | Inv. No. | Accts. Rec. Dr | Sales Bicycles Cr | Sales Dolls Cr |
|------|------|----------|----------------|-------------------|----------------|
| 8 3 | Seth Roberts | 516 | 10 95 ✓ | | 10 95 |
| 5 | Bill's Repair Shop | 517 | 5 95 ✓ | | |
| 10 | Cycle Service | 518 | 32 50 ✓ | | |
| 15 | Dale Roberts | 519 | 157 00 ✓ | 157 00 | |
| 17 | Bill's Repair Shop | 520 | 113 49 ✓ | 113 49 | |
| 20 | Grant Cole | 521 | 65 23 ✓ | | 65 23 |
| 25 | Henry Andrews | 522 | 55 00 ✓ | | |
| 31 | Lambert's Toy Store | 523 | 512 00 ✓ | | |
| | Totals | | 952 12 | 270 49 | 76 18 |
| | | | Dr # 101 ✓ | Cr # 300 ✓ | Cr # 301 ✓ |

| Sales Toys Cr | Sales Misc. Cr | | | | |
|---------------|----------------|---|---|---|---|
| | 5 95 | | | | |
| 32 50 | | | | | |
| | | | | | |
| | | | | | |
| 55 00 | | | | | |
| 512 00 | | | | | |
| 599 50 | 5 95 | | | | |
| Cr # 302 ✓ | Cr # 303 ✓ | | | | |

6

The total of each sales invoice is entered into the column accounts receivable. From this column we post the amounts to the customers' accounts in the accounts receivable ledger being sure to place a check mark (√) by the side of the amount as it is posted and show the posting reference (such as SJ49). By distributing the sales items to the different columns it will give the company an idea of how many bicycles, dolls, toys, etc. were sold. At the end of each month the sales journal is totaled and the totals are posted to their respective accounts in the General Ledger.

At this point, there is one very important thing to note. In the accounts receivable ledger we post each separate invoice to the customers' accounts. In the General Ledger we post the total of the invoices for the month. This is how control of the posting work is maintained. If you add all amounts in the accounts receivable ledger, the total should equal the amount of the accounts receivable page in the General Ledger. This is how you know your work was done accurately. If these amounts don't agree, then you must go back and recheck your postings to find the mistake.

Let us summarize what we have just covered.
1. The Sales Journal is used for recording sales of merchandise on account and to show sales information on items sold.
2. From the Sales Journal, the amount of each invoice is posted to the customers' page in the accounts receivable ledger.
3. At the end of each month the columns are added, balancing the debits and the credits.
The totals are posted to their respective accounts in the General Ledger.

### PRACTICE PROBLEMS

To test your understanding of the Sales Journal we are listing some transactions to be entered on the blank illustrations by following the three steps we have just given you.

1. Aug 1.—Inv. No. 238—George Hays, Inc. bought on account—4 tires for                    $125.00

2. Aug. 8—Inv. No. 312—Troy's Handy Service bought on account—3 batteries                    75.00

3. Aug 15—Inv. No. 421—Chuck Rodgers bought on account—10 fan belts                    20.00

4. Aug. 20—Inv. No. 475—Leslie Keith bought on account—1 set seat covers                    25.00

STEP 1. Record the transactions to the Sales Journal.

|  |  |  |  |  |  |
|---|---|---|---|---|---|
|  |  |  |  |  |  |
|  |  |  |  |  |  |
|  |  |  |  |  |  |
|  |  |  |  |  |  |
|  |  |  |  |  |  |
|  |  |  |  |  |  |
|  |  |  |  |  |  |
|  |  |  |  |  |  |

|  |  |  |  |  |  |  |  |  |  |
|--|--|--|--|--|--|--|--|--|--|
|  |  |  |  |  |  |  |  |  |  |
|  |  |  |  |  |  |  |  |  |  |
|  |  |  |  |  |  |  |  |  |  |
|  |  |  |  |  |  |  |  |  |  |
|  |  |  |  |  |  |  |  |  |  |
|  |  |  |  |  |  |  |  |  |  |
|  |  |  |  |  |  |  |  |  |  |
|  |  |  |  |  |  |  |  |  |  |

**STEP 2.** Open accounts in the accounts receivable ledger and post to them from the sales journal.

|  |  |  |  |  |  |  |  |  |
|--|--|--|--|--|--|--|--|--|
|  |  |  |  |  |  |  |  |  |
|  |  |  |  |  |  |  |  |  |
|  |  |  |  |  |  |  |  |  |
|  |  |  |  |  |  |  |  |  |
|  |  |  |  |  |  |  |  |  |
|  |  |  |  |  |  |  |  |  |
|  |  |  |  |  |  |  |  |  |

|  |  |  |  |  |  |  |  |  |  |  |  |
|--|--|--|--|--|--|--|--|--|--|--|--|
|  |  |  |  |  |  |  |  |  |  |  |  |
|  |  |  |  |  |  |  |  |  |  |  |  |
|  |  |  |  |  |  |  |  |  |  |  |  |
|  |  |  |  |  |  |  |  |  |  |  |  |
|  |  |  |  |  |  |  |  |  |  |  |  |
|  |  |  |  |  |  |  |  |  |  |  |  |
|  |  |  |  |  |  |  |  |  |  |  |  |
|  |  |  |  |  |  |  |  |  |  |  |  |
|  |  |  |  |  |  |  |  |  |  |  |  |

STEP 3. Open accounts in the general ledger. Total the columns in the sales journal and post the totals to the accounts opened in the general ledger.

|  |  |  |  |  |  |  |  |  |  |  |  |
|--|--|--|--|--|--|--|--|--|--|--|--|
|  |  |  |  |  |  |  |  |  |  |  |  |
|  |  |  |  |  |  |  |  |  |  |  |  |
|  |  |  |  |  |  |  |  |  |  |  |  |
|  |  |  |  |  |  |  |  |  |  |  |  |
|  |  |  |  |  |  |  |  |  |  |  |  |
|  |  |  |  |  |  |  |  |  |  |  |  |
|  |  |  |  |  |  |  |  |  |  |  |  |
|  |  |  |  |  |  |  |  |  |  |  |  |
|  |  |  |  |  |  |  |  |  |  |  |  |

# CHAPTER IV
## CASH RECEIPTS JOURNAL

The Cash Receipts Journal is a record of all cash (checks, money orders, etc.) received for payment on accounts and/or sales of merchandise. These payments and sales should be recorded daily after which a deposit is made in the Company's bank.

The Cash Receipts Journal usually consists of the very basic information which is listed in detail.
1. Date—when cash is received.
2. Item—is for explaining what the cash is for; i.e. a cash sale or a customers payment on account in which case you enter the customers name as it appears in the Accounts Receivable Ledger.
3. Invoice Number—The customer may have several invoices charged to his account and a record by number will identify each purchase.
5. Accounts Receivable—is for entering the amount to be credited to the customers account. The figures in this column will then be posted as a credit to the respective customer's account and a check made by the side of the amount to show it has been posted.
6. Sales—for entering cash sales.
7. Cash Discount—is for entering the discount allowed to the customer for paying his account within a specified time.

The following illustration will show you how the seven steps just given are put to use.

| CR 26 | | | | Cash Receipt Journal | | | | | |
|---|---|---|---|---|---|---|---|---|---|
| | | | | August, '19___ | | | | | |
| Date | | Item | Inv No. | Cash Received Dr | | Accounts Receivable Cr | | Misc Sales Cr | |
| 8 | 1 | Sales | | 22 | 50 | | | 22 | 50 |
| | 5 | Sales | | 115 | 00 | | | 115 | 00 |
| | 10 | John Allen | 468 | 58 | 80 | 60 | 00 ✓ | | |
| | 20 | Sales | | 7 | 23 | | | 7 | 23 |
| | 20 | Bill's Repair Shop | 520 | 50 | 00 | 50 | 00 ✓ | | |
| | 30 | Mary Davis | 430 | 15 | 60 | 15 | 60 ✓ | | |
| | | Totals | | 269 | 13 | 125 | 60 | 144 | 73 |
| | | | | Dr #100 ✓ | | Cr #101 ✓ | | Cr #303 ✓ | |

| Disc allowed Dr | | | | | | Deposits in Bank | | | |
|---|---|---|---|---|---|---|---|---|---|
| | | | | | | 137 | 50 | | |
| 1 | 20 | | | | | 58 | 80 | | |
| | | | | | | 57 | 23 | | |
| | | | | | | 15 | 60 | | |
| 1 | 20 | | | | | 269 | 13 | | |

Dr #404

In bookkeeping all pages are numbered, just as they are in all books, but with the exception that you use the initials of the Journal you are working in and start the first page of each Journal with Number 1.  As you will note by our illustration we have CR26. This means Cash Receipt page 26. At the beginning of each fiscal year start the page numbers over again.

At the end of the month the columns are added and the totals balanced across. By balancing, we mean all the debits equal all the credits. If and when the columns are balanced enter the totals to the General Ledger being sure to enter the debits as debits and the credits as credits.

Let's look back and sum up this Cash Receipts Journal.

1. All cash receipts and payments entered to this book.
2. From this book, the customers' payments are posted as a credit on their account sheet in the Accounts Receivable Ledger.
3. At the end of each month the columns in the Cash Receipts Journal are added and the totals are posted in the General Ledger where a separate sheet is kept for each such as;
   a. Cash Receipts total posted as a debit to the Bank Account
   b. Accounts Receivable total posted as a credit to the Accounts Receivable account
   c. Sales totals are posted as a credit to the respective sales accounts
   d. Discount allowed total posted as a debit to discount allowed account
   e. The deposits column is for record only to show the day's receipts were deposited in the bank

## PRACTICE PROBLEMS

We are listing some transactions to be entered on the blank illustrations to test your understanding of the Cash Receipts Journal. Follow the steps we have just given you.

1. Aug. 10—Misc. cash sales $10.25

2. Aug. 20—Inv. No. 238—George Hays, Inc. paid on account 75.00

3. Aug. 25—Misc. cash sales 32.00

4. Aug. 30—Inv. No. 421—Chuck Rodgers paid on account 20.00

STEP 1. Record the transactions to the cash receipts journal.

STEP 2. Post credits to the accounts receivable ledger accounts.
STEP 3. Open accounts in the General Ledger. Total the columns in the cash receipt journal and post totals to the proper accounts in the general ledger.

# CHAPTER V

## PURCHASE JOURNAL

The Purchase Journal is used for recording purchases made on account for

1. Merchandise for resale to customers
2. Supplies for use in conducting the business
3. Plant assets

Because of the variety of assets acquired on credit terms, the purchase journal should be designed to accomodate the recording of everything purchased on account. The number and the purpose of special columns provided in the Journal depend upon the nature of the business and the frequency of purchases of the various assets.

For each transaction recorded in the purchase journal, the credit is entered in the Accounts Payable credit column. The next columns are used in accumulating debits to the particular accounts most frequently affected.

From the purchase journal we post to each creditor's account in the Accounts Payable Ledger making a check mark (√) by the side of the amount to show it has been posted. (per illustration). As you will note the entries to the Accounts Payable creditors sheet will be in the credit column and the balances shown in red ink or with brackets around them.

Usually bills and statements from the creditor's are received at the first of the month and are payable by the 10th of the month. It is a good practice to wait until all the statements or bills are in (providing they are in by the 5th or 6th of the month) and then alphabetize them according to the creditor's name. This system makes it easier to find information if needed; also, the Accounts Payable is already in alphabetical order and it makes it better and easier for posting.

It is wise to check and read the statements that are received looking for any errors before entering them. If you do not receive a statement and have a lot of bills from one creditor run an adding machine tape and staple it to the bills. This makes it easier to write the check for it later on.

When the bills have been received and alphabetized, they are ready to enter into the Purchase Journal in the month for which the purchase was made.

The following information is needed when setting up the purchase journal sheet.

1. Date of bill
2. Name of creditor
3. Amount of bill
4. Distribution of item

At the time the bill is entered in the purchase journal place the PJ number on the bill to show that it was entered. Keep all the bills in the same order so that when the check is written for it, the check number can be placed on it also, and then the bills are ready for filing.

After the bills have been entered and the columns totaled and balanced, the totals of the columns are posted to the General Ledger, where there is an account sheet for each. The miscellaneous column accounts will have to be posted separately instead of the total being posted.

Study the following illustration showing how the purchase journal is set up.

| PJ 8 | | Purchase Journal August, 1969 | | Accts. Pay. Cr | | Utilities Dr | | Office Supplies Dr | |
|---|---|---|---|---|---|---|---|---|---|
| Date | | | | | | | | | |
| 1969 8 31 | City Electric | | | 48 | 23 ✓ | 48 | 23 | | |
| 31 | Loto Insurance Co. | | | 95 | 70 ✓ | | | | |
| 31 | Missy Doll Store | | | 169 | 75 ✓ | | | | |
| 31 | Office Supply Co. | | | 53 | 50 ✓ | | | 53 | 50 |
| 31 | Scott Repair Service | | | 23 | 00 ✓ | | | | |
| 31 | Trotter Cycle Shop | | | 186 | 00 ✓ | | | | |
| 31 | Walcott Toy Co. | | | 359 | 50 ✓ | | | | |
| 31 | Water Dept. | | | 15 | 20 ✓ | 15 | 20 | | |
| | Totals | | | 950 | 88 | 63 | 43 | 53 | 50 |
| | | | | CR #200 ✓ | | Dr #403 ✓ | | Dr #401 ✓ | |

Second half of ledger sheet on page 20 _____

Second half

| Purchases Bicycles Dr | Purchases Dolls Dr | Purchases Toys Dr | Miscellaneous Acct - | | Dr |
|---|---|---|---|---|---|
| | | | Bldg. Ins. | 95 70 | ✓ |
| | 169 75 | | | | |
| | | | Equip. Repair | 23 00 | ✓ |
| 186 00 | | | | | |
| | | 359 50 | | | |
| 186 00 | 169 75 | 359 50 | | 118 70 | |

Dr #201 ✓    Dr #202 ✓    Dr #203 ✓

Now to summarize: the purchase journal is used for entering bills received from creditors for merchandise purchased and expenses incurred. From this book, we post to each creditor's account in the accounts payable ledger. The totals of each column are posted to the General Ledger.

## PRACTICE PROBLEMS

We are listing some transactions to be entered on the blank forms by following the steps we have given you.

1. Aug. 31—Invoice from Pierce Tires for 2 tires          $ 40.00

2. Aug. 31—Invoice from Taylor Gas Co. for 100 gallons gas     41.00

3. Aug. 31—Invoice from Bates Belt Co. for 12 fan belts       12.00

4. Aug. 31—Invoice from Ace Tire Co. for 4 tires          100.00

# STEP 1. Enter the invoices received to the Purchase Journal.

| | | | | | | | | | |
|---|---|---|---|---|---|---|---|---|---|
| | | | | | | | | | |
| | | | | | | | | | |
| | | | | | | | | | |
| | | | | | | | | | |
| | | | | | | | | | |
| | | | | | | | | | |
| | | | | | | | | | |
| | | | | | | | | | |
| | | | | | | | | | |
| | | | | | | | | | |
| | | | | | | | | | |

| | | | | | | | | |
|---|---|---|---|---|---|---|---|---|
| | | | | | | | | |
| | | | | | | | | |
| | | | | | | | | |
| | | | | | | | | |
| | | | | | | | | |
| | | | | | | | | |
| | | | | | | | | |
| | | | | | | | | |
| | | | | | | | | |
| | | | | | | | | |

STEP 2. Open accounts in the accounts payable ledger and post to them from the Purchase Journal.

|  |  |  |  |  |  |
|--|--|--|--|--|--|
|  |  |  |  |  |  |
|  |  |  |  |  |  |
|  |  |  |  |  |  |
|  |  |  |  |  |  |
|  |  |  |  |  |  |
|  |  |  |  |  |  |
|  |  |  |  |  |  |
|  |  |  |  |  |  |

|  |  |  |  |  |  |
|--|--|--|--|--|--|
|  |  |  |  |  |  |
|  |  |  |  |  |  |
|  |  |  |  |  |  |
|  |  |  |  |  |  |
|  |  |  |  |  |  |
|  |  |  |  |  |  |
|  |  |  |  |  |  |
|  |  |  |  |  |  |

STEP 3. Open accounts that are needed in the General Ledger. Total the columns in the Purchase Journal and post the totals to the proper accounts in the General Ledger.

|  |  |  |  |  |
|---|---|---|---|---|
|  |  |  |  |  |
|  |  |  |  |  |
|  |  |  |  |  |
|  |  |  |  |  |
|  |  |  |  |  |
|  |  |  |  |  |
|  |  |  |  |  |
|  |  |  |  |  |

|  |  |  |  |  |
|---|---|---|---|---|
|  |  |  |  |  |
|  |  |  |  |  |
|  |  |  |  |  |
|  |  |  |  |  |
|  |  |  |  |  |
|  |  |  |  |  |
|  |  |  |  |  |
|  |  |  |  |  |

# CHAPTER VI

## CASH DISBURSEMENTS JOURNAL

The Cash Disbursements Journal is a book for entering the checks written and distributing the cost or expense to the right accounts. The Cash Disbursements Journal should have the following information.

1. Date check written
2. Name of whom check was written to
3. Check number
4. Amount of check
5. Distribution of expense

When a check is written the stub of the check should be properly filled out in order that the information can be relayed to the Cash Disbursement Journal. Enter from the check stub or voucher to the cash disbursement journal daily so that a close examination can be kept on the bank balance. Make a check mark on the stub signifying it has been entered. Enter the checks in numerical order and for the amount of the check—do not guess—it must be correct.

If a check is written in payment of an account with a creditor this amount should be distributed first to the amount of check column and then to the accounts payable column. The figures in the accounts payable column are posted to the creditor's sheet in the acounts payable ledger as a debit and then subtracted from the balance. Make a check (√) by the side of the figures as they are posted.

If you are paying an expense item that has not been entered in the accounts payable distribute it to the expense column set up for it. There may not be enough columns on your sheet to set up a column for each expense so set up a miscellaneous column as per illustration on page 27.

The columns are added up at the end of the month and balanced. The totals are entered in the General Ledger to the accounts provided.

**Study the following illustration.**

| | | | | | | |
|---|---|---|---|---|---|---|
| CD8 | | | | | | |

Cash Disbursements Journal
September, 1969

| Date | | | Ck No. | Amount of Check Cr | Accounts Payable Dr | Payroll Dr |
|---|---|---|---|---|---|---|
| 9 | 10 | City Electric | 251 | 48 23 | 48 23 | |
| | 10 | Loto Insurance Co | 252 | 95 70 | 95 70 | |
| | 10 | Missy Doll Store | 253 | 169 75 | 169 75 | |
| | 10 | Office Supply Co | 254 | 53 50 | 53 50 | |
| | 10 | Scott Repair Service | 255 | 23 00 | 23 00 | |
| | 10 | Trotter Cycle Shop | 256 | 186 00 | 186 00 | |
| | 10 | Walcott Jay Co. | 257 | 359 50 | 359 50 | |
| | 10 | Water Dept. | 258 | 15 20 | 15 20 | |
| | | Totals Forwarded | | 950 88 | 950 88 | |

| Taxes Cr | Travel Expense Dr | | Miscellaneous Acct - | Dr |
|---|---|---|---|---|
| | | | | |
| | | | | |
| | | | | |
| | | | | |
| | | | | |
| | | | | |
| | | | | |

| CB9 | Cash Disbursements Journal September, 1969 | | | | |
|---|---|---|---|---|---|

| Date | | Ck No | Amount of check Cr | Accounts Payable Dr | Payroll Dr |
|---|---|---|---|---|---|
| | Balance Forwarded | | 950 88 | 950 88 | |
| 9 15 | George Conner | 259 | 175 03 | | 190 00 |
| 15 | Alice Timms | 260 | 67 50 | | 80 00 |
| 15 | Joe Black | 261 | 93 15 | | 115 00 |
| 20 | George's Repair | 262 | 5 75 | | |
| 30 | George Conner | 263 | 175 03 | | 190 00 |
| 30 | Alice Timms | 264 | 67 50 | | 80 00 |
| 30 | Joe Black | 265 | 93 15 | | 115 00 |
| | Totals | | 1627 99 | 950 88 | 770 00 |
| | | | Cr #100 ✓ | Dr #200 ✓ | Dr #400 ✓ |

| Taxes Dr | Travel Expense Dr | | | Miscellaneous acct - | Dr |
|---|---|---|---|---|---|
| 14 97 | | | | | |
| 12 50 | | | | | |
| 21 85 | | | | | |
| | | | | Office Equip Repair | 5 75 ✓ |
| 14 97 | | | | | |
| 12 50 | | | | | |
| 21 85 | | | | | |
| 98 64 | | | | | 5 75 |
| Cr #407 ✓ ✓ | | | | | |

28

As you will note by studying the illustrations, more than one page was needed, so add the columns on each page as they are filled and carry the totals forward to the next page, etc. until the end of the month.

At the end of the month the totals will then be posted to the General Ledger where there is a sheet for each account needed.

The Cash Disbursements Journal is used when figuring the bank reconciliation (Page # 35 ).

Summarize:

1. Checks are entered numerically in the amount of check column and distributed to one of the columns, depending on what it is for.
2. The accounts payable is posted to the creditor's account in the accounts payable ledger as a debit.
3. At the end of the month, the columns are added and balanced.

The totals are posted to the General Ledger, where there is a separate account sheet for each.

## PRACTICE PROBLEMS

We are submitting some transactions to test your understanding of the Cash Disbursements Journal. Use the blank forms provided and follow the steps we have given you.

1. Aug. 5—Check No. 981 to City Water Dept. for utilities     $ 10.00

2. Aug. 10—Check No. 982 to Taylor Gas Co. for
   payment on tccount °     25.00

3. Aug. 15—Check No. 983 to Paul Little for commissions
   on sales     120.00

4. Aug. 15—Check No. 984 to Rice Repair Shop
   for payment on account     7.50

STEP 1. Enter the checks written in the Cash Disbursement Journal.

STEP 2. Post to accounts in the accounts payable ledger.
STEP 3. Open accounts that are needed in the General Ledger. Total columns in the Cash Disbursements Journal and post the totals to the proper accounts in the General Ledger.

## CHAPTER VII

## GENERAL JOURNAL

The General Journal is the book where entries are made when they cannot be entered in the Journals mentioned in the previous chapters. This Journal is used for entering any corrections to errors that have been made; to record a transaction such as sale of equipment or property; to record taxes that have not been set up; to record the accounts to be closed out at the end of the year to Profit & Loss.

Any transaction can be entered in this book and should be clearly stated what the entry is for. Each entry is posted separately to the General Ledger to the account given and a check mark (√) made when posted. (Per Illustration).

| | | | | | | | | |
|---|---|---|---|---|---|---|---|---|
| DJ 6 | | | *General Journal* | | | | | |

| Date | Explanation | Acct No. | Debit | | | Credit | | |
|---|---|---|---|---|---|---|---|---|
| 8 31 | Office Supplies | 401 | 25 00 | √ | | | | |
| | Postage | 402 | | | | 25 00 | √ | |
| | "To correct entry | | | | | | | |
| | originally made | | | | | | | |
| | in the wrong | | | | | | | |
| | column." | | | | | | | |

# CHAPTER VIII

## PAYROLL JOURNAL

It is of the utmost importance to keep payroll records no matter how small the business. All of this is necessary in order to fill out Federal Quarterly Report Forms and the Annual W-2 Form.

Except for certain types of employment, all employers are required to withhold a portion of the earnings of their employees for payment of the employees' liability for federal income tax. The amount required to be withheld varies in accordance with the amount of earnings and the number of exemptions. An employee may claim an exemption for himself, for each person who qualifies as a dependent, such as his children, and for his wife unless she is also employed and claims her own exemption. Every employee is required by law to file with his employer an employee's withholding exemption certificate in which he reports the number of his exemptions.

Example of W-4 form shown:

---

**FORM W-4** (Rev. Jan. 1967)
U.S. Treasury Department
Internal Revenue Service

### EMPLOYEE'S WITHHOLDING EXEMPTION CERTIFICATE

Type or print full name _____  Social Security Number _____

Home address _____  City _____  State _____  ZIP code _____

**EMPLOYEE:**
File this form with your employer. Otherwise, he must withhold U.S. income tax from your wages without exemption.

**EMPLOYER:**
Keep this certificate with your records. If the employee is believed to have claimed too many exemptions, the District Director should be so advised.

**HOW TO CLAIM YOUR WITHHOLDING EXEMPTIONS**

1. If SINGLE (or if married and wish withholding as single person), write "1." If you claim no exemptions, write "0". . . . _____
2. If MARRIED, one exemption each is allowable for husband and wife if not claimed on another certificate.
   (a) If you claim both of these exemptions, write "2"; (b) If you claim one of these exemptions, write "1"; (c) If you claim neither of these exemptions, write "0" . . . . . . . . . . . . _____
3. Exemptions for age and blindness (applicable only to you and your wife but not to dependents):
   (a) If you or your wife will be 65 years of age or older at the end of the year, and you claim this exemption, write "1"; If both will be 65 or older, and you claim both of these exemptions, write "2" . . . . . . . . . .
   (b) If you or your wife are blind, and you claim this exemption, write "1"; If both are blind, and you claim both of these exemptions, write "2" . . . . . . . . . . . . . . . . . . _____
4. If you claim exemptions for one or more dependents, write the number of such exemptions. (Do not claim exemption for a dependent unless you are qualified under Instruction 4 on other side.). . . . . . . . . . . _____
5. If you claim additional withholding allowances for itemized deductions fill out and attach Schedule A (Form W-4), and enter the number of allowances claimed (if claimed file new Form W-4 each year) . . . . . . . . . . _____
6. Add the exemptions and allowances (if any) which you have claimed above and write total . . . . . . . . . [      ]
7. Additional withholding per pay period under agreement with employer. (See Instruction 1.) . . . . . . . . $ _____

I CERTIFY that the number of withholding exemptions claimed on this certificate does not exceed the number to which I am entitled.    o48—16—79061-1

(Date) _____, 19____    (Signed) _____

---

The amount of social security tax and withholding tax to be withheld from the employee's earnings can be determined by a withholding table issued by the Internal Revenue Service free of charge. They come in payroll periods such as weekly, biweekly, semimonthly and monthly.

There may be other deductions involved also such as; group insurance, savings bonds, etc.

At the time the employee is hired and he has filled out the W-4 form an individual record should be made showing his name and address, social security number, number of dependents claimed and his rate of pay.

Some employees work on a straight salary basis while others work by the hour. There is no problem in figuring the straight salary as it remains the same every week.

The salary of those on an hourly basis is determined as follows:
1. First add up the hours worked as shown on the time card.
2. Multiply the number of hours worked by the rate per hour. The result is the gross amount earned. If the employee's time card reveals he worked overtime( which is time worked over 40 hours in one week) his earnings should be figured as follows basing he worked 8 hours overtime and earns $3.00 per hour.

| | |
|---|---:|
| Earnings at base rate—40 hours x $3.00= | $120.00 |
| Earnings at overtime rate—8 hours x $4.50 (1½ times) | 36.00 |
| | ——— |
| Total earnings | $156.00 |

The employee's deductions should now be deducted to get his net pay.

The individual payroll records are totaled quarterly in order to figure the Federal Quarterly Report. At the end of the year, all quarters are totaled on the individual payroll records to figure the W-2 forms.

---

1

**WAGE AND TAX STATEMENT 1969**

Copy A—For Internal Revenue Service

Type or print EMPLOYER'S identification number, name, and address above.

| FEDERAL INCOME TAX INFORMATION | | | SOCIAL SECURITY INFORMATION | | |
|---|---|---|---|---|---|
| Federal income tax withheld | Wages paid subject to withholding in 1969 [3] | Other compensation paid in 1969 [2] | F.I.C.A. employee tax withheld [3] | Total F.I.C.A. wages paid in 1969 [4] | |

EMPLOYEE'S social security number ▶

[1] Includes tips reported by employee. Amount is before payroll deductions or sick pay exclusion.

[2] Report salary or other employee compensation which was not subject to withholding. See Circular E. Farmers, see Circular A.

[3] One-eighth of this amount was withheld to finance the cost of Hospital Insurance Benefits. The remainder is for old-age, survivors, and disability insurance.

[4] Includes tips reported by employee.

Type or print EMPLOYEE'S name and address (including ZIP code) above.

Uncollected Employee Tax on Tips . . . . $

FORM **W-2** U.S. Treasury Department, Internal Revenue Service    16—80183-1    **EMPLOYER:** See instructions on back of copy D.

34

# CHAPTER IX
# BANK RECONCILIATION

The bank reconciliation is for reconciling the bank statement with the bank balance in the General Ledger at the end of each month.

When the bank statement is received with the cancelled checks, (1) place the checks in numerical order (2) make a check mark (√) by the check numbers, in the Cash Disbursements Journal, of the checks that are cancelled (3) make a list of all the checks that have not come in showing the check number and amount. Total the amounts of the checks and this will give you the figure of all outstanding checks (checks not yet cashed at the bank).

The following is a sample of reconciling the bank account:

| | |
|---|---:|
| Ending balance on bank statement | $1,000.00 |
| Plus: Deposit made on August 31 not shown on statement | 250.00 |
| Less: Outstanding checks per list | 135.00 |
| Bank balance | $1,115.00 |

| | |
|---|---:|
| Bank balance—(7-31-69) | $2,321.50 |
| Plus: Deposits for month (from cash receipts journal and deposit slips) | 5,809.25 |
| Less: Checks written for month (from cash disbursements journal) | 7,015.75 |
| Book balance (8-31-69) (Same figure as shown in General Ledger on bank account page). | $1,115.00 |

As you will note this shows the book figure balances with the bank statement figure.

Keep your reconciliation for the next month to check off the outstanding checks you have just listed.

## CHAPTER X

## GENERAL LEDGER

Now that you have learned all about the Journals and what goes into them let us now go on to the final step. We must compile all our efforts into one book for the final information we are seeking. From this book our financial statements are prepared.

There should be a page in the General Ledger for each account needed. You may set up as many as you have need of. The General Ledger account sheets consist of the Assets, Liabilities, Income and Expense.

We are illustrating how the accounts will appear in the General Ledger. These accounts are taken from the illustrations that are shown in the previous chapters. For the sake of simplicity, we are not showing all of the accounts and are omitting all postings from the beginning of the year to August 1.

At the end of the month, the totals from each column in the Journals are posted to the General Ledger. The accounts are balanced and this is done by adding all the debits, adding all the credits, subtracting the small amount from the larger and writing the difference in the balance column. When there is a credit balance show it in red ink or brackets around it. Every page should have a balance total if there has been any entries made on it. When the balances are finished, an adding machine tape should be run on the balances on each page, adding in the debits and subtracting the credits. When you are finished running the tape you should have a -0- total. If there shows a balance, a mistake has been made which must be found by rechecking all postings until the error is found.

Examples of the General Ledger set up is as follows:

| 100 | Bank | | | | |
|---|---|---|---|---|---|
| Date | | Post Ref. | Debit | Credit | Balance |
| 8 1 | Balance | | | | 2015 75 |
| 8 31 | | CR26 | 269 13 | | |
| 9 30 | | CD9 | | 1627 99 | 656 89 |

## 101     Accounts Receivable

| Date | | Post Ref. | Debit | Credit | Balance |
|---|---|---|---|---|---|
| 8 31 | | SJ 49 | 952 12 | | |
| 8 31 | | CR 26 | | 125 60 | 826 52 |
| | | | | | |

## 200     Accounts Payable

| Date | | Post Ref | Debit | Credit | Balance |
|---|---|---|---|---|---|
| 8 31 | | PJ 8 | | 950 88 | |
| 9 30 | | CD 9 | 950 88 | | — 0 — |
| | | | | | |

## 300     Sales - Bicycles

| Date | | Post Ref | Debit | Credit | Balance |
|---|---|---|---|---|---|
| 8 31 | | SJ 49 | | 270 49 | ⟨270 49⟩ |
| | | | | | |
| | | | | | |

| 400 | | | Payroll | | |
|---|---|---|---|---|---|
| Date | | Post Ref | Debit | Credit | Balance |
| 9 30 | | 089 | 770 00 | | 770 00 |
| | | | | | |
| | | | | | |
| | | | | | |

| 401 | | | Office Supplies | | |
|---|---|---|---|---|---|
| Date | | Post Ref | Debit | Credit | Balance |
| 8 31 | | Pg 3 | 53 50 | | |
| 31 | | Pg 6 | 25 00 | | 78 50 |
| | | | | | |
| | | | | | |

## TRIAL BALANCE

After all the Journals have been posted to the General Ledger and after each account in the General Ledger is balanced, a trial balance can be prepared. A trial balance is a testing of the account balances, with all debits in one column and all credits in another.

After all the debits and the credits have been listed, add both columns. The total of both must be the same, hence, this proves the General Ledger is in balance. A financial statement may be prepared from the trial balance.

## CHAPTER XI

## SIMPLE BOOKKEEPING

In the previous chapters we have discussed a method of bookkeeping that is applicable for all size of business operations. The very small to the very large organizations can use the system we have just covered.

There are some businesses and housewives who may wish to keep records of their income and expenses without keeping a full set of books. This chapter is designed especially to help those people.

The purpose of keeping records is to determine the income and expense which can provide all necessary information into just one book. All transactions can be entered on one page each month. At the end of the month, the totals may be posted to one page which will provide information for the entire year.

The book the transactions will be entered in is called the Journal. The page that the monthly totals are posted to is called the Ledger.

The Journal will consist of several columns and should be headed up to suit the needs.

We are illustrating the use of the Journal.

| | Income | | | | Expense | | |
|---|---|---|---|---|---|---|---|
| January, 19___ | | | | | | | |
| Date | Cash Received | Sales | Misc Sales | Date | Amount Paid Out | Purchases | Misc Expenses |
| Jan 1 | 25 00 | 25 00 | | Jan 1 | 3 95 | | 3 95 |
| 2 | 115 00 | 110 00 | 5 00 | 5 | 15 00 | 15 00 | |
| 5 | 350 00 | 350 00 | | 10 | 100 00 | 100 00 | |
| 10 | 290 00 | 290 00 | | 10 | 22 00 | 22 00 | |
| 15 | 73 50 | 70 00 | 3 50 | 15 | 90 00 | | 90 00 |
| 20 | 106 00 | 106 00 | | 31 | 75 00 | 75 00 | |
| 30 | 210 00 | 210 00 | | | | | |
| Totals | 1169 50 | 1161 00 | 8 50 | Totals | 305 95 | 212 00 | 93 95 |

# SUMMARIZE

As you will note, the amounts in the income column represent the income received during the month. This may be income from sales, rents, fees, royalties, etc. The entries should be made each day.

The total amount received each day should be entered in the Cash Received column and distributed to the Sales column (or any other column you have set up).

The expense column should be entered each day also. The total expense each day is entered in the Amount Paid Out column and the amount distributed to columns set up to handle what the expense is for. The columns may be altered to suit any particular need. Such as, the housewife may have income such as from salaries, rent, royalties, etc. and her expenses would be rent, food, car expense, clothing, insurance, etc. The most important thing is that a column be set up for the frequent income and expenses. A miscellaneous column can be set up for the incidentals.

After all the transactions have been entered, each column is added and the totals written in at the bottom of each column. These totals are then posted to the page which we call the Ledger. There should be a separate column for each item set up on this page.

We are submitting some illustrations of the Ledger after posting from the Journal.

Ledger - Year of _____

| | Income | | | | Expenses | | |
|---|---|---|---|---|---|---|---|
| | Cash Received | Sales | Misc Sales | | Amount Paid Out | Purchases | Misc Expenses |
| January | 1169 50 | 1161 00 | 8 50 | January | 305 95 | 212 00 | 93 95 |
| February | | | | February | | | |
| March | | | | March | | | |
| April | | | | April | | | |
| May | | | | May | | | |
| June | | | | June | | | |

By having all this information accumulated on one page, it is easy to figure the income tax return. At the end of the year, the columns are added up and the totals of each column are entered at the bottom of each column.

## CHAPTER XII

## BUDGETNG METHOD

The housewife will find that keeping a budget is rewarding and helpful. It need not be a chore. If it is kept up regularly, it will not be a burden. Keeping up with the income and expenses of the household can be made real simple by using the form that is provided.

| January Income | | | | | January Expenses | | | | |
|---|---|---|---|---|---|---|---|---|---|
| Date | Total | Salaries | Royalties | Other | Date | Total | Rent | Food | Other |
| | | | | | | | | | |
| | | | | | | | | | |
| | | | | | | | | | |
| | | | | | | | | | |
| | | | | | | | | | |
| | | | | | | | | | |
| | | | | | | | | | |

At the end of each month the items are totaled and the totals transferred to a page (in a tablet or anything you might have) such as:

| | Income | | | | | Expenses | | | |
|---|---|---|---|---|---|---|---|---|---|
| | Salaries | Royalties | Fees | Other | | Rent | Food | Clothing | Other |
| January February March | | | | | January February March | | | | |
| | | | | | | | | | |
| | | | | | | | | | |
| | | | | | | | | | |
| | | | | | | | | | |
| | | | | | | | | | |
| | | | | | | | | | |

At the end of each month transfer these totals to a comparison budget sheet and get a good look at how your money was spent.

| Budget for January, 19— | | | | | | |
|---|---|---|---|---|---|---|
| | Total | Rent | Food | Clothing | Auto | Misc. |
| Budget | | | | | | |
| Amt. Spent | | | | | | |
| Over Budget | | | | | | |
| Under Budget | | | | | | |

A budget system will depend solely on your circumstances and will work effectively only if it is used everyday. It can help you to plan for the future.

NOW

FOR YOUR

BONUS

## CREATE YOUR OWN BUSINESS FORMS AND STATIONERY

There are many ways of obtaining business forms. "Adequate" is a law to many business people . . . so, choose forms which serve well at minimum expense. The following pages are actual FORMS which your printer can reproduce with your name and address. Convert your business card into a letterhead, paste-in copy on the chosen forms, and pay a visit to your local photo-offset printer. Make sure it is a photo-offset shop.

**FOR EXAMPLE:** Cut your business card up with a pair of scissors so that each line of copy is separated—then, rearrange the copy into the desired order and glue it down in the position that you desire on the bookkeeping business form of your choice.

*Educator Books, Inc.*

PUBLISHERS OF PAPERBACKS
AND HARDCOVERS ON
MOST SUBJECTS
*"We Specialize in Reprints"*
TELEPHONE 915 / 655-3296

P.O. DRAWER 32          SAN ANGELO, TEXAS 76901

↓

*Educator Books, Inc.*

P.O. DRAWER 32    TELEPHONE 915 / 655-3296       SAN ANGELO, TEXAS 76901

↓

ORDER FORM

*Educator Books, Inc.*
DRAWER 32 SAN ANGELO, TEXAS 76901

SPECIAL INTEREST
CUSTOM BOUND PAPERBACKS

| Quantity | NAME OF BOOK | Paperback | Total | Cloth | Total |
|---|---|---|---|---|---|
| | BOTTLE COLLECTOR'S HANDBOOK AND PRICING GUIDE | $3.95 | | $6.95 | |
| | BARBED WIRE HANDBOOK AND PRICING GUIDE | $3.95 | | $5.95 | |
| | P OK OF C CTI | $2.00 | | $6.00 | |
| | W TO B/ ME A OFESSIONAL JEY BF E PL R | $2.98 | | $5.95 | |
| | TO TH LAS! | .98 | | $5.9 | |
| | S RA | | 5 | 6. | |

45

STATEMENT

# YOUR ADDRESS HERE

## ( CITY )  ,_____ 19 ___

_____

_____

| DATE | | DEBITS | CREDITS | BALANCE |
|------|--|--------|---------|---------|
| | | | | |
| | | | | |
| | | | | |
| | | | | |
| | | | | |
| | | | | |
| | | | | |
| | | | | |
| | | | | |
| | | | | |
| | | | | |
| | | | | |
| | | | | |
| | | | | |
| | | | | |
| | | | | |
| | | | | |
| | | | | |

STATEMENT

_____19 __

_____

_____

IN ACCOUNT WITH

# YOUR ADDRESS HERE

| DATE | DESCRIPTION | CHARGES | CREDITS | BALANCE |
|------|-------------|---------|---------|---------|
| | | BALANCE FORWARD | | |
| | | | | |
| | | | | |
| | | | | |
| | | | | |
| | | | | |
| | | | | |
| | | | | |
| | | | | |
| | | | | |
| | | | | |
| | | | | |
| | | | | |
| | | | | |
| | | | | |
| | | | | |
| | | | | |
| | | | | |

YOUR ADDRESS HERE

NAME_____  DATE_____

ADDRESS_____  PHONE_____

TOWN_____  DATE
                                      WANTED_____

| ESTIMATE OF MATERIAL AND LABOR | MATERIAL | | LABOR | |
|---|---|---|---|---|
| | | | | |
| | | | | |
| | | | | |
| | | | | |
| | | | | |
| | | | | |
| | | | | |
| | | | | |
| | | | | |
| | | | | |
| | | | | |
| | | | | |
| | | | | |
| | | | | |
| | | | | |
| | | | | |
| | | | | |
| | | | | |
| | | | | |
| | | | | |
| TOTALS | | | | |
| GRAND TOTAL | | | | |

## ESTIMATE SHEET AND REPAIR ORDER

THIS ESTIMATE IS BASED ON OUR INSPECTION AND DOES NOT COVER ADDITIONAL MATERIAL OR
LABOR WHICH MAY BE REQUIRED AFTER THE WORK HAS BEEN STARTED. AFTER THE WORK HAS
STARTED, DAMAGED MATERIAL WHICH WAS NOT EVIDENT ON FIRST INSPECTION MAY BE DIS-
COVERED. NATURALLY THIS ESTIMATE CANNOT COVER SUCH CONTINGENCIES. THIS ESTIMATE
IS FOR IMMEDIATE ACCEPTANCE.

AUTHORIZED BY_____

48

# YOUR ADDRESS HERE

## ( CITY) ,_____19 __

NAME_____

ADDRESS_____

| MAKE OF CAR | LICENSE No. | SPEEDOMETER | TIME WANTED | | |
|---|---|---|---|---|---|
| SERVICE OR PRODUCT | | | | WORKMAN | AMOUNT |
| GALLONS | GASOLINE @ | | | | |
| QUARTS | OIL @ | | | | |
| GALLONS | KEROSENE @ | | | | |
| CHASSIS LUBRICATION | | | | | |
| CHANGE ENGINE OIL | | | | | |
| CHANGE TRANS. F.W. DIFF. | | | | | |
| LUBRICATE FRONT WHEELS | | | | | |
| LUBRICATE SPRINGS | | | | | |
| WASH SIMONIZE | | | | | |
| DRAIN AND SERVICE WET CLUTCH | | | | | |
| LUBRICATE CLUTCH THROWOUT BEARING | | | | | |
| QUARTS | | | | | |
| TIRE WORK | | | | | |
| BATTERY | | | | | |
| MISCELLANEOUS | | | | | |
| | | | | | |
| | | | | | |
| | | | | | |
| YOUR ATTENTION IS CALLED TO: | | | | | |

49

YOUR ADDRESS HERE

NAME _____ DATE _____ 19____

ADDRESS _____ PHONE

| LICENSE NO. & STATE | MAKE & MODEL | MOTOR NO. | SERIAL NO. | MILEAGE |
|---|---|---|---|---|

| OPER. NO. | KIND OF WORK | AMOUNT |
|---|---|---|

| QUAN. | PART NO. | ARTICLE | PRICE |
|---|---|---|---|

GALS. GAS @

QTS. OIL @

LBS. GREASE @

TOTAL

| QUAN. | Accessories, Tires & Tubes | PRICE |
|---|---|---|

TOTAL

| | |
|---|---|
| TOTAL LABOR | |
| TOTAL PARTS | |
| GAS, OIL, GREASE | |
| ACCESSORIES | |
| TIRES, TUBES | |
| OUTSIDE REPAIRS | |
| TAX | |
| TOTAL | |

I hereby authorize repair work to be done as described above with necessary parts, to be listed at your regular prices. I agree to pay cash on delivery of car or on satisfactory terms to you; and until paid in full it shall constitute a lien on this car. I further agree that you will not be held responsible for car or articles left in car in case of fire, theft, accidents or other causes beyond your control. My car may be driven by your employees for road tests at my own risk.

| PROMISED | DELIVERED | WORK AUTHORIZED BY | RECEIVED BY |
|---|---|---|---|

50

NAME_____ DATE_____ 19____

ADDRESS_____ PHONE_____

| ITEM | SERIAL NO. | MOTOR NO. | DATE PICKED-UP | DATE WANTED |
|------|-----------|-----------|----------------|-------------|

KIND OF WORK — AMOUNT

LABOR

PARTS

TAX

TOTAL

I hereby authorize repair work to be done as described above with necessary parts, to be listed at your regular prices. I agree to pay cash on delivery or on satisfactory terms to you; and until paid in full it shall constitute a lien on the above listed item. I further agree that you will not be held responsible for articles left, in case of fire, theft, or other causes beyond our control.

AUTHORIZED BY _____ | RECEIVED BY _____

| QUAN. | PART NO. | ARTICLE | PRICE |
|-------|----------|---------|-------|

PARTS

51

SOLD TO

ADDRESS

CITY

SHIPPED TO

DATE

ORDER NO.

SHIPPED

SALES TAX NO.

| PART NO. | DESCRIPTION | CODE | M'N'FR | QUAN. | UNIT PRICE | | AMOUNT |
|---|---|---|---|---|---|---|---|
| | | | | | LIST | NET | |
| | | | | | | | |
| | | | | | | | |
| | | | | | | | |
| | | | | | | | |
| | | | | | | | |
| | | | | | | | |
| | | | | | | | |
| | | | | | | | |
| | | | | | | | |
| | | | | | | | |
| | | | | | | | |

TERMS NET

NET TOTAL

BY

| CREDIT | STOCK | INVOICE | SHIP | PRICE | EXTEND | CHECK | LOCATION |
|---|---|---|---|---|---|---|---|
| | | | | | | | |

52

| CUSTOMER'S ORDER NO. | | | | DATE | | | |
|---|---|---|---|---|---|---|---|

19

NAME

ADDRESS

| SOLD BY | CASH | C. O. D. | CHARGE | ON ACCT. | MDSE. RETD. | PAID OUT | |
|---|---|---|---|---|---|---|---|

| QUANTITY | DESCRIPTION | | PRICE | | AMOUNT | |
|---|---|---|---|---|---|---|
| | | | | | | |
| | | | | | | |
| | | | | | | |
| | | | | | | |
| | | | | | | |
| | | | | | | |
| | | | | | | |
| | | | | | | |
| | | | | | | |
| | | | | | | |
| | | | | | | |
| | | | | | | |
| | | | | | | |
| | | | | | | |
| | | **TAX** | | | | |
| | | **TOTAL** | | | | |

No. _____ Rec'd by

_____19 __

FOR SERVICES RENDERED

PAID ON ACCOUNT

BALANCE DUE

RECEIVED PAYMENT_____

# TELEVISION SERVICE ORDER

| | |
|---|---|
| YOUR ADDRESS HERE | DATE OF ORDER |
| | DATE PROMISED |

| NAME | | TEL. NO. |
|---|---|---|
| ADDRESS | APT. NO. | CITY |

☐ PARTS WARRANTY  ☐ CONTRACT SERVICE  CONTRACT EXPIRES    ☐ C. O. D.  ☐ ESTIMATE

| TYPE & MAKE | MODEL | SERIAL NO. | REPAIRED IN: ☐ HOME  ☐ SHOP |
|---|---|---|---|

☐ TV  ☐ ANT.  ☐ RADIO  ☐ SERVICE  ☐ PICK-UP  ☐ DELIVER

**NATURE OF SERVICE REQUEST**

| QUAN. | PART NO. | PARTS DESCRIPTION | | PRICE |
|---|---|---|---|---|
| | | | | |
| | | | | |
| | | | | |
| | | | | |
| | | | | |
| | | | | |
| | | | | |
| | | | | |

| RECEPTION | | | | | | | | | | | | | | | |
|---|---|---|---|---|---|---|---|---|---|---|---|---|---|---|---|
| CHANNEL | 1 | 2 | 3 | 4 | 5 | 6 | 7 | 8 | 9 | 10 | 11 | 12 | 13 | **PARTS** | |
| REC. | | | | | | | | | | | | | | | |

KEY:    G-GOOD    F-FAIR    P-POOR    **TAX**

LABOR NOTES:    **LABOR**

COMMENTS:    **SERVICE CHARGE**

**TOTAL**

TECHNICIAN _____    CUSTOMER'S SIGNATURE _____

55

Received of _____

$ _____

_____

_____

_____ 19 ___

_____

_____ DOLLARS

No. ___

Received of _____

$ _____

_____

_____

_____ 19 ___

_____

_____ DOLLARS

56

No.———— DATE———— 19 ———

Received of————

FOR————

————DOLLARS

$————

---

No.———— DATE———— 19 ———

Received of————

FOR————

————DOLLARS

$————

---

No.———— DATE———— 19 ———

Received of————

FOR————

————DOLLARS

$————

---

No.———— DATE———— 19 ———

Received of————

FOR————

————DOLLARS

$————